YOGA, POWER, and SPIRIT

Also by Alberto Villoldo, Ph.D.

THE FOUR INSIGHTS*

DANCE OF THE FOUR WINDS (with Erik Jendresen)

THE FIRST STORY EVER TOLD

HEALING STATES (with Stanley Krippner, Ph.D.)

ISLAND OF THE SUN (with Erik Jendresen)

MENDING THE PAST AND HEALING
THE FUTURE WITH SOUL RETRIEVAL*

MILLENNIUM GLIMPSES INTO THE 21ST CENTURY

THE REALMS OF HEALING (with Stanley Krippner, Ph.D.)

SHAMAN, HEALER, SAGE

*Available from Hay House

❀ ❀ ❀

Please visit Hay House USA: **www.hayhouse.com**®
Hay House Australia: **www.hayhouse.com.au**
Hay House UK: **www.hayhouse.co.uk**
Hay House South Africa: **orders@psdprom.co.za**
Hay House India: **www.hayhouseindia.co.in**

YOGA, POWER, and SPIRIT

Patanjali the Shaman

Alberto Villoldo, Ph.D.

HAY HOUSE, INC.
Carlsbad, California
London • Sydney • Johannesburg
Vancouver • Hong Kong • New Delhi

Published and distributed in the United States by: Hay House, Inc.: www.
hayhouse.com • ***Published and distributed in Australia by:*** Hay House
Australia Pty. Ltd.: www.hayhouse.com.au • ***Published and distributed in the
United Kingdom by:*** Hay House UK, Ltd.: www.hayhouse.co.uk • ***Published
and distributed in the Republic of South Africa by:*** Hay House SA (Pty),
Ltd.: orders@psdprom.co.za • ***Distributed in Canada by:*** Raincoast: www.
raincoast.com • ***Published in India by:*** Hay House Publishers India: www.
hayhouseindia.co.in

Editorial supervision: Jill Kramer • *Design:* Tricia Breidenthal

Library of Congress Cataloging-in-Publication Data

Villoldo, Alberto.
  Yoga, power, and spirit : Patanjali the Shaman / Alberto Villoldo. -- 1st ed.
     p. cm.
  Includes bibliographical references.
  ISBN-13: 978-1-4019-1047-1 (hardcover) 1. Yoga. 2. Patañjali. Yogasutra.
I. Title.
  B132.Y6V466 2007
  181'.452--dc22
                              2006025389

ISBN: 978-1-4019-1047-1

10 09 08 07   4 3 2 1
1st edition, April 2007

To La Loba,
Keeper of Dreams

Alberto offers a poetic and transformative translation of the Yoga Sutras that breathes life and radiance into Patanjali's wisdom in a way that is thankfully different, but complementary to other scholarly translations.

— Shiva Rea

Alberto's poetic and inspired interpretation of these sacred treasures spoke directly to my heart. I recommend them to every seeker on the Path.

— Deva Premal

CONTENTS

INTRODUCTION

Praise the Mother Goddess

he Ganges bursts out from a glacial spring high in the Himalayas, two-thirds of the way up Mt. Shivling, at an icy outcropping known to the locals as Gaumukh, or "the mouth of the cow." I had hiked for several days to pray at the source of the Holy River, near where the Yoga Sutras had been put to parchment some 2,500 years earlier by a sage named Patanjali. As I climbed, I observed the *sadhus,* the pilgrim yogis, sitting in stoic meditation and bathing in the frigid waters. Then, at a point nearly 13,000 feet above sea level, I took off my shoes and tested the water with my toes. I concentrated on my breath, and immersed myself.

> Breathe in,
> breathe out,
> breathe in.

A few moments later, I sensed myself hovering above the stream and observed my body below me, shivering silently. I remembered what Patanjali had written about the yogi being able to leave his body at will. I felt free and unbounded; and could perceive the snowcapped mountains around me, the forest below, and the vast expanse of blue sky above that both enveloped and held me. I was perceiving all of this at once. Nature and river and sky and I were one.

Then, something drew my awareness back to my body. In a flash, I was back in my own skin and let go a yell that echoed through the mountains. I leaped out of the stream, and as the circulation returned to my limbs, my body felt as if it were being pricked by a million tiny icicles. I sprawled on a large boulder, laughing and crying, soaking up its warmth. I reminded myself that yoga is an inner practice, and that braving ice and fire is fine, but the real tests of the yogi are spiritual.

I had come to the source of the Ganges to research this book. I was also here to ask for a blessing from Devi, the Mother Goddess, to compose a version of Patanjali's Sutras that brought forth the juicy, feminine, and non-dogmatic wisdom of this ancient tradition. I've spent many years practicing yoga, as well as studying with the sages of the Americas. In the Yoga Sutras, I found many parallels to what I'd discovered among indigenous shamans I'd met halfway around the world. Both yogis and shamans sought to master levels of consciousness that would help them break free from suffering and bring them to a direct and immediate experience of the

Divine. Both sought stillness and enlightenment and the expression of their fullest human potential. Both sought to heal themselves through their discipline and practice. The more I learned about the ancient yogis who had lived thousands of years ago in the foothills of the Himalayas, the more I came to realize that these yogis were the ancestors of the shamans of Tibet and the Americas. Their descendants were the men and women who settled the snow-capped mountains, entered Siberia, and later crossed the Bering Strait into America.

In my experience, the Yoga Sutras had become fossilized and stagnant, the interpretations bogged down in a masculine, dogmatic, priestly tradition. Returning to the source of these teachings, I felt encouraged to bring forth a version of the Yoga Sutras that celebrated the feminine and more direct path to Spirit, one that was informed by and pollinated with the poetry and beauty of the primordial wisdom of its authors.

There are many scholarly translations of the Yoga Sutras. This is not one. This is an interpretative version. It is meant for the traveler seeking to explore a more feminine path to Spirit. There is a long tradition of reinterpretation by the followers of the sramanic stream of yoga, which included Prince Siddhartha. The *sramans* (a name that would perhaps evolve into *shaman* in Siberia) were wandering yogis who did not subscribe to the rigid Vedic laws that discriminated on the basis of caste, gender, and degree of scholarly learning. These men and women believed that the infinite Self could be experienced only by direct realization, and that freedom and immortality could be attained in a single lifetime.

The most renowned yogi of the sramanic stream was Buddha, who as a young man (Siddhartha) left the comfort and wealth of the palace to become a wandering yogi. He believed that the priestly tradition and caste system deviated from the eternal truths that were available to everyone.

The icy lesson I learned at the headwaters of the Ganges was the sign I had been waiting for, reassuring me that Devi approved of my intention to breathe new life into the eternal wisdom that is at the foundation of the Sutras. I felt that the waters of the Ganges had delivered me like the waters of a mother that gush forth at the moment of birth.

This version of the Yoga Sutras takes us back to the source of yoga and its original teachings about the mind; the yogic powers, or *siddhis:* and the direct experience of Spirit. It recalls the time when yoga was practiced along the banks of the Ganges and the Sarasvati rivers. And it is based on the premise that yoga is the source of the shamanic wisdom of the Americas.

The Origins

Shamanism is an archaic technique of ecstasy still practiced by countless peoples around the world. The word *shaman* derives from the Siberian term for a man or woman who mediates between the visible world of humans and the invisible worlds of energy and spirit. Just as shamans do, the Yoga Sutras advocate a knowledge that is experiential and personal. The word *yoga* derives from the Sanskrit word *yuj,* meaning "to yoke or join"; and refers to the awakening to our nature as Spirit, which we experience when we practice yoga and lift ourselves out of mundane consciousness. Through yoga practice, we awaken to our Self, which exists beyond the ego or personality, beyond the self with a small *s.*

The Yoga Sutras describe experiences that are universal yet must be discovered and rediscovered by each one of us. To teach us this wisdom, Patanjali employs the ancient format known as the *sutra,* a succinct aphorism that lends itself easily to memory, and could therefore be transmitted orally. The word *sutra* literally means "thread"; and while Patanjali provides us with the wool, we must spin it and weave it into our own tapestry—one that's personal and yet has a pattern recognizable to all who share the yogic experience. The sutra is a densely packed verse that must be "unpacked" by the practitioner, interpreted using the skills and wisdom acquired through her experiences of yoga rather than through the teachings of someone else or the knowledge contained in a book. This is a traditional style of learning common to yoga, and found in Buddhism as well as shamanism. Buddhism relies on the yogic methods of contemplation and meditation, and the principles of nonattachment and dis-identification with ego.

The Yoga Sutras

Patanjali compiled a practical guide to the techniques of ecstasy and liberation, but yoga's sources certainly existed long before Patanjali. In the Bhagavad-Gita, written 500 years before the Yoga Sutras were composed, Krishna reveals the eternal yoga to Arjuna. He explains that this yoga is ancient, and that he'd revealed it earlier to the sages of old, who conveyed it to the wise *rishi* kings.

While it's sometimes possible to determine the date when a manuscript was written, it's impossible to establish a date for the origin of the ideas themselves. In all likelihood, the system of yoga comes from a very ancient tradition that was concerned with the question of what survives after death: *What is the immortal aspect of man?* The practices described by the Yoga Sutras lead the seeker to answer this and other questions through personal experience.

According to lore, yoga wasn't discovered incrementally, one bit of knowledge at a time, but received by the ancient sages in its totality. Sutra I:24-26 states:

> *Spirit taught the greatest teachers directly.*
> *Spirit dwells in timelessness*
> *free from the past*
> *free from the future.*

Very little is known about Patanjali himself. Some scholars claim he lived in the first or second century B.C.E. while others believe he lived as late as the 5th century of the Christian era. It's also possible that Patanjali was a mythical character altogether, as is suggested by his name, which means a gift from heaven that falls into the open palms of the yogi.

The Yoga Sutras are made up of four books. The first one consists of 51 aphorisms (sutras) and is the book on yogic ecstasy, or *samadhi*. It provides the theory and philosophy of yoga. The second is the book on realization, or the practice of yoga, and contains 55 sutras. The third, which has 55 aphorisms, reveals the yogic powers, or *siddhis*. The fourth book, which has only 34 verses, seems to be a later addition to the Patanjali text. It is on absolute freedom, and repeats many of the points made in the earlier books.

Patanjali reinterpreted yoga at a time when it was becoming obfuscated, when the earlier teachings had been replaced by codified religious practices and arcane ritual. And while the wisdom of yoga was woven into the texts and beliefs of Hinduism, a central point differentiates yoga from mainstream Hinduism. In yoga, it's said that the world exists and is real; while in Vedanta, the world is *maya,* or an illusion. The ancient ways of yoga acknowledge the soil and fruit of the Mother Earth and the feminine aspect of the Divine, of Devi.

The Great Goddess

Long before patriarchal religions took hold among ancient people, the feminine aspect of the Divine was revered. In India, the earliest historical reference to the Great Goddess comes from the city of Mohenjo-daro in northern India, where her cult was prevalent.

The earliest yogis lived in nomadic groups and were drawn to the rivers where food was abundant and water was never in short supply. These societies honored the earth for her bounty and riches, and worshiped the Divine Mother along the banks of the Ganges, Yamuna, and Sarasvati rivers. The Sarasvati River has long since disappeared as a result of shifts in tectonic plates, but archaeologists continue to discover the remnants of ancient civilizations that flourished along its banks. Over thousands of years, these people developed a culture that was highly refined. They had an extensive understanding of mathematics and astronomy, and their architecture was astonishingly sophisticated. Indeed, new archeological discoveries are causing us to reconsider the history of India. Postcolonial investigators are even pondering whether the land of seven rivers, in northwest India, where the Sarasvati culture arose, might be the true cradle of Western civilization, and not Mesopotamia, as was previously thought.

Devi, the Divine Mother, was revered as the creative principle of the universe. She is the Goddess, the primal force of nature and fertility. She brings the waters from heaven and protects humans. She is the mother of life and death, holding joy and pain in her right hand, life and death in her left. The universe is contained in her womb. In her fiercest forms, Devi is known as Durgha and Kali; while in her most tender expressions, she is Lakshmi, or Parvati. She resides in all women as the animating force in a woman's soul.

But around the time that oral traditions were codified into religious texts the beliefs and practices of ancient people began to shift. Priests were appointed and hierarchies created, and rules and dogma instituted. With the appearance of the Vedas, access to the Divine became increasingly guarded by a caste of male priests who interpreted the holy texts. The feminine aspect of Spirit, Devi, began to be pushed aside. This began to translate as a disdainful attitude toward women as well, as is evident in modern India. Even the Bhagavad-Gita says:

"Those who take refuge in me, Arjuna,
even if they are born in evil wombs,
as women or laborers or servants,
also reach the supreme goal."
(9:32) (Version by Steven Mitchell)

In the Divine Mother's temples of old, she would receive offerings of blood: women's menstrual blood, and the blood of animals sacrificed to her as the Goddess of life and death. Today, Devi's most powerful forms have been eclipsed by her image as the consort to Shiva (in her role as Parvati), mother to Ganesh, or wife to Vishnu (in her role as Lakshmi). Worshipers no longer bring her offerings of blood; they bring her sweets and jewelry. The sacred feminine is to be appeased with trinkets.

After the appearance of the Vedas, Devi was no longer portrayed as the one who battles demons, but as the consummate nurse or lover. The Goddess began to lose her place of power as an equal to the God, and she became the wife or mother, subordinate to the masculine aspect of Divinity. Later, as she migrated to Europe, she even began to be demonized. The English word *devil* is hauntingly similar to *Devi*.

In India, this erosion of feminine power has been not just symbolic, but also literal. The Rig Veda, the oldest of the Vedas, censures women, saying,

"Indra himself hath said,
The mind of woman brooks not discipline.
Her intellect hath little weight."
(Rig Veda 8/33/17)

Until recently, women in India couldn't own property. And while legislation in India regarding child marriages and dowries is changing, the burning of brides by in-laws who consider their dowries insufficient, as well as other traditions that harm and dishonor women, linger. Even the path of the *sadhu* is mostly closed to women, and 90 percent of these renunciate yogis are men. The female *sadhus* are mostly widows who would otherwise be outcasts.

Slowly, however, women in India, and around the world, are beginning to reclaim their power and Divinity, the Devi that resides deep within them. And people everywhere are starting to reject the idea that the only path to bliss is through adherence to rituals and rules, and immersion in dusty tomes filled with someone else's stories.

Yoga and Shamanism

While many books on yoga have been written by yogis, very few books on shamanism have been written by shamans. Thus scholars believed that yoga and shamanism were very different practices. Scholars claimed that for the yogi, achieving *samadhi,* the state of bliss, involves focusing the mind on a single point and completely mastering one's self, while shamans merely attain *ecstasy,* a euphoric state in which the ego dissolves but which doesn't lead to the shaman achieving mastery of the self. While this is still a popular notion about shamanism, it is incorrect. My own fieldwork with the high shamans of the Americas has shown me that the goals of yoga and shamanism are identical.

The dismissal of yoga and shamanism as primitive mysticism is a glaring example of colonial anthropology. We know that history is written from the perspective of the conqueror, and not through the eyes of the vanquished. Thus, the spiritual practices of indigenous Americans have been written off as unsophisticated, when in reality, these civilizations were in many ways more advanced than those of the European conquerors. At the time of the Spanish Conquest, for example, there were more than 125,000 citizens living in Teotihuacán, Mexico, in a spotlessly clean city with running water and sanitation; while less than 100,000 people lived in London, largely in squalor.

This colonial, superior attitude was also applied to India. Take, for example, the belief that the Vedas were written by invading Aryan peoples who brought their sophisticated ways to India. Those who subscribe to this theory argue that such a brilliant piece of literature, called by the German philosopher Hegel "the starting point for the whole Western world," couldn't have been authored by dark-skinned Indians from the subcontinent. Today, postcolonial scholars are discovering that there may have never been an Aryan invasion of India, that the theory was probably concocted, based on scant evidence gathered by colonial historians during the occupation of India by the British. Similarly, it was only after Margaret Mead and other modern investigators began discovering the vast richness and complexity of the spiritual traditions of the Americas and other parts of the world that these types of assumptions about "primitive" people began to change. Now, we can look at shamanism and yoga and see what they have in common.

Like the yogis, shamans go through a death of the ego: They cease to identify with their body and the impermanent world, and discover their true nature as Spirit. The lore of India describes saints who were able to fly through the air, yogis who could travel across great distances in an instant, and who could appear and disappear at will. The Hindu legends speak of *rishis* who possessed the power of flight. Patanjali describes these powers to travel through time and space in Sutra III:46:

Embracing these powers
mastering the elements
traveling through time and space
the yogi can fashion a new body for himself
one that ages, heals, and dies differently.

The magical flight is meant to be taken both literally and metaphorically. The Sutras are referring to the yogi's ability to break free of the trappings of the body at any time—not only at the moment of death—and to journey to the heavenly planes to receive the gifts of Divine knowledge directly. The soul flight is a metaphor for the yogi's ability to attain liberation from the bonds of karma and the material world. This is one reason why the Yoga Sutras are such a powerful body of teaching, because they say that you don't need a guru or a priest mediating between you and Spirit. A guru can be a guide, but you must never give your power over to him. You must undertake your own journey with courage, discipline, and audacity, and all will be bestowed upon you.

The mastery of fire is a central theme of many yogic and shamanic practices. The fire refers to the intense heat produced by awakening the Kundalini, the dormant *Shakti* energy within each of us. In certain Indo-Tibetan initiatory ceremonies, a monk is required to dry a large number of wet sheets placed on his naked body during a snowy winter night by releasing the fire inside him.

Yoga and shamanism share many other similarities as well, as you shall see.

Freedom from the Confines of Time, Karma, and History

Both the yogi and the shaman do away with their past and the ties that keep them bound to their karmic and family histories. They also learn to break free of time to taste infinity; and in doing so, reach an unconditioned, natural state where they recover their "original Self."

The ideal state of the yogi is freedom, or *jivamukta*, becoming one who is "liberated in life." The yogi has broken free from the grip of his personal history. He lives in the eternal present. After the death of the ego, the yogi no longer possesses an individual consciousness—he does nothing, and nothing ever happens to him. His only consciousness is as a witness. Nothing can fetter him to this world, because his acts have no consequence. No matter what he does, he will accrue no karma. Although the shaman may not use the word *karma*, he too aims to break free of the haunting stories of the past and the need to continue reliving them. For the shaman, as the yogi, in order to heal, stubborn identities must be shed and personal histories drained of their power.

Simple Practices Instead of Elaborate Rituals

In both yoga and shamanism, excessive and elaborate rituals are abhorred. In Hinduism, by contrast, there are religious rituals for everything. There is a ceremony for a baby's first visit to a temple or first feeding with solid food, and even a ritual that involves the expectant father parting a pregnant mother's hair three times in order to ensure the growing embryo's health. In yoga, no such rituals are required. The practices are simple: *pranayama,* or the deep, cyclic breathing associated with meditation; *asana,* or posture; and *ekagrata,* or "single mind." All of these practices bring together the elements of our fragmented existence and connect us to Spirit.

Experiential Knowledge, Not Secondhand Wisdom

Shamanism recognizes the importance of the individual having his own, unique experience of Spirit. The Laika, the ancient shamans of the Andes, believed that the teachings of their priests were stories that were helpful for understanding someone else's encounter with the sacred, but not a replacement for encountering Spirit directly. Similarly, Patanjali did away with the hierarchies of priests, temples, and even with the notion of the guru and of God itself. The Yoga Sutras tell us to look within, to practice *pratyahara* (turning within) and experience *samadhi* (the state of bliss). Patanjali brings us the personal practices that will lead to the immediate experience of Spirit.

While Vedanta holds all power in contempt, the Yoga Sutras prescribe both awakening and employing the spiritual powers, or *siddhis,* to attain supreme freedom. Patanjali understood that these powers are simply a means to liberation, and not a goal in themselves. Attaining spiritual powers is inevitable, because they appear naturally and spontaneously as one makes progress in the path of yoga. The *siddhis* are essential to achieving *samadhi,* which is the true power.

Patanjali tells us that these powers are "perfections" of the human condition ("perfection" is the original meaning of the word *siddhi*). To deny them is to deny your ultimate freedom. You can only step beyond these powers once you've acquired them. Renouncing them beforehand, as many practitioners of yoga do, mimics yet forestalls the true liberation.

In addition, renouncing the *siddhis,* as some yoga teachers today advocate, keeps you powerless, and perpetuates your suffering as a victim. The masculine paradigm insists that these powers must be used only by the few, the privileged—namely, the priests. The feminine way of yoga says we should all embrace the *siddhis,* flex our spiritual muscles, and step beyond time and form to experience freedom from karma.

Not even God's help is needed in this process. While Patanjali accepts the existence of Isvara, the Lord, he does not attribute any great importance to him. Isvara is not the creator of the world, and he is not involved in all of human endeavors. He is the lord of yogis only, and can only assist those who have chosen the path of yoga. He has no personality, being neither vengeful nor forgiving. Instead, Isvara is pure Spirit, never having entered the stream of time or karma; and can't be influenced by faith, rituals, or devotion. Rather than being a heavenly parent, Isvara is simply a model of who the yogi can become. The yogi attempts to be as Isvara in the world, without becoming absorbed by it or meddling with it in any way.

Breaking Free of the Trappings of the Mind

Yoga defines the problem of our human existence very concretely. We suffer because we confuse the mind for the Spirit, the ego for the Self. Freedom can only be obtained by resolving this mix-up, first by understanding the nature of the mind, and then by achieving the immediate experience of Spirit, or our True Self. Patanjali explains that freedom can't be attained through study or learning. It is ours only when we enter timelessness and taste infinity. To do so requires breaking free of the trappings of the material world, and our minds.

Yoga expounds on the importance of renunciation of the material world and our attachments to it. At the source of the Ganges River, I met many *sadhus*—the renunciate yogis who wander throughout the holy places of India. These men own nothing and spend their lives walking, most often barefoot, in pilgrimage. They carry only a water jar, which reminds them that at any time, they can dip their cup into the waters of wisdom, represented by the river Ganges, and taste infinity.

Yet even the yogis who are not *sadhus* teach about renunciation, explaining that while you can renounce outer possessions, giving up your belongings, it's even more important to renounce inner possessions, such as your judgments, thoughts, values, and notions about right and wrong. They are on an inner pilgrimage, carrying an inner water jar, and they urge others to follow the path. Their teachings are ancient, and they're captured in the Yoga Sutras. But renunciation by itself can become an addiction. As Swami Venkatesananda said: "Rennouce the self that does the renunciation."

The Promise of Yoga

Over millennia, yoga was developed as a set of tools for releasing one from suffering, and achieving a state in which the human and Divine come together, where one can embody both being and nonbeing, eternity and death. The Yoga Sutras provide step-by-step instructions for attaining the yogic experience of pure being, in which one's consciousness is unfettered, and with it, all suffering that accompanies the human condition is transcended.

Yogis discovered methods for acquiring liberation from the endless cycle of birth and death within a single lifetime. It's said that the soul inhabits many different bodies over the course of many successive lifetimes, continually experiencing suffering. Using the practices of yoga, we can achieve full divinity and free ourselves from the pain of working through the unending karma of millennia.

The methods of yoga that Patanjali explains include many techniques—posture, breathing, meditation, and spiritual powers. But all forms of yoga share a common thread, which is to take us out of a profane existence and into a sacred relationship with life. We live a profane life when we simply do what is expected of us, striving to create what our culture considers a proper life in the material world, unconscious of our spiritual nature. The rhythm of such a life is hectic, hurried, and restless, in contrast to the sacred life, which is lived in contemplation and meditation, according to one's own natural rhythm.

Confronted by the manic pace of everyday life, the yogi slows down, takes a deep breath, and practices *pranayama,* breathing deeply and learning to focus on a single point instead of multitasking. He responds to the beckoning of the material world with a smile, and withdraws to the inner world of spirit and grace.

The only path available to the yogi is renouncing the ways of greed, fear, and materialism in order to live according to the ways of heaven. This doesn't mean that he doesn't hold a job or raise a family or enjoy abundance. It means that he performs his tasks in the world consciously, knowing that his True Self is much greater than the limited definition of selfhood that any of these aspects of the everyday life can offer him.

Thus, the yogi begins to wake up from the cultural trance that we've all been educated into. She begins by renouncing her identification with the most mundane aspects of living—the distractions and relationships that waste her time and dissipate her energies. She then seeks to yoke, or bring together, the most important elements of the sacred life, including a healthy diet, clean water and air, meditation, *asana*, right relationships, and the practice of nonviolence.

Patanjali states that when we practice yoga, we can acquire extraordinary abilities that will help us wake up from our cultural trance. When we're willing to become a master of our own journey, the *siddhis* are inevitable. We can achieve *samadhi* and regain our original nature, as well as the singularity of knowledge available before the visible and invisible worlds parted. Then we understand that Spirit is everywhere, that only our flawed vision prevents us from seeing this. From then on, for the yogi, every act is sacred. Everything we do is a form of worship.

Like the ancient yogis, we can all rediscover the sacred. We can all practice yoga and begin our journey toward *samadhi,* toward liberation.

— Alberto Villoldo, Ph.D.
www.thefourwinds.com

SAMADHI,
OR
YOGIC
ECSTASY

Before time
Before space
   the teachings of yoga took form.

❦ ❦ ❦

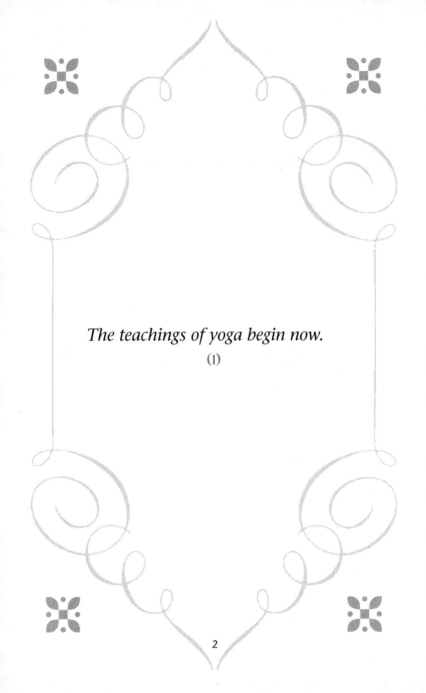

The teachings of yoga begin now.

(1)

*Yoga is vigilance, awareness,
  and stillness of the mind.*

*Yoga frees you
    from the drama,
    the tragedy, the saga
    your mind creates
    and allows you to
    experience your True Self.*

(2 ε 3)

Your True Self knows
reality and does not confuse it
with the twisted tales your mind spins.
Some of these stories bring pleasure;
some bring pain.

All are forms of fiction that distract
you from reality and your True Self.

(3, 4, 5)

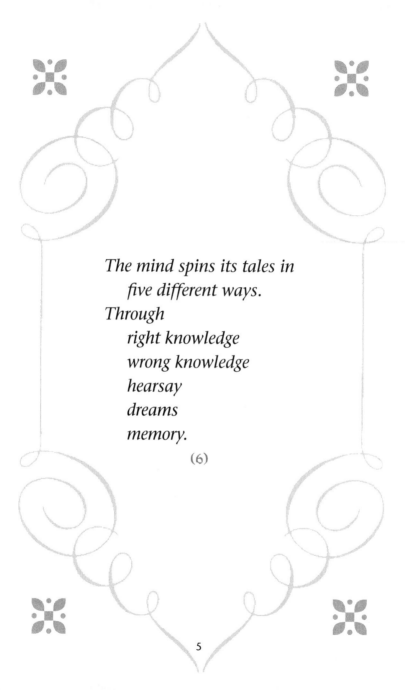

The mind spins its tales in
*   five different ways.*
Through
*   right knowledge*
*   wrong knowledge*
*   hearsay*
*   dreams*
*   memory.*

(6)

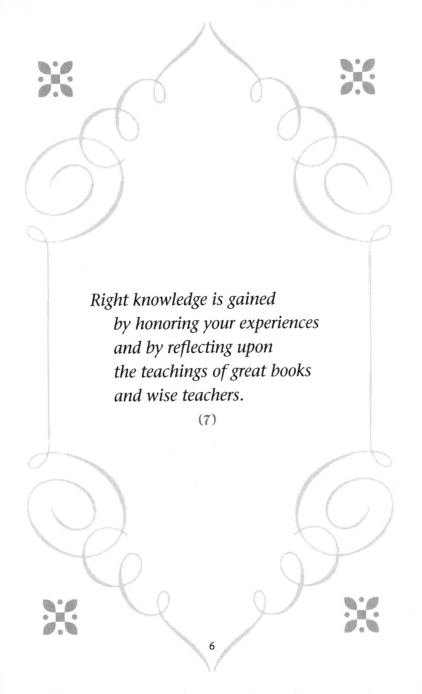

Right knowledge is gained
by honoring your experiences
and by reflecting upon
the teachings of great books
and wise teachers.

(7)

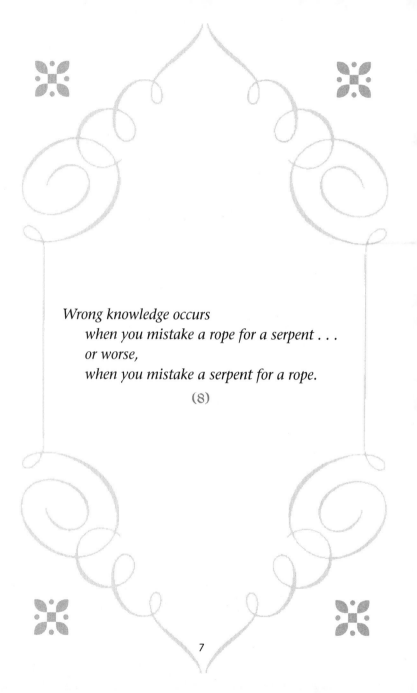

Wrong knowledge occurs
   when you mistake a rope for a serpent . . .
   or worse,
   when you mistake a serpent for a rope.

(8)

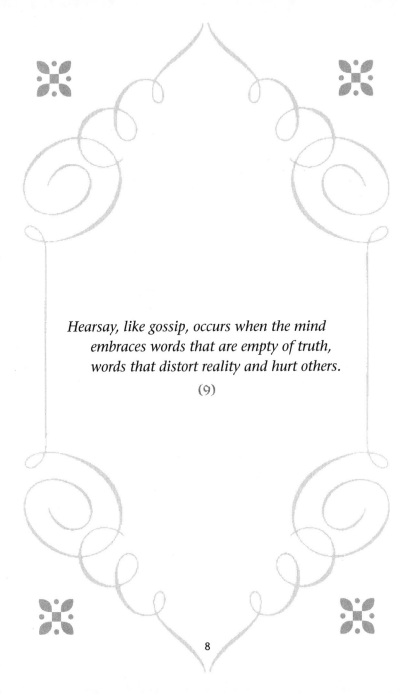

Hearsay, like gossip, occurs when the mind embraces words that are empty of truth, words that distort reality and hurt others.

(9)

In the deepest dream,
    you speak with your father
    who has passed away.
You travel to distant lands.
You play the flute and sing
    yet have no musical talent.

Later, you taste the
    waters of nothingness,
    as all thought,
    all emotion,
    all sensation
    cease.

(10)

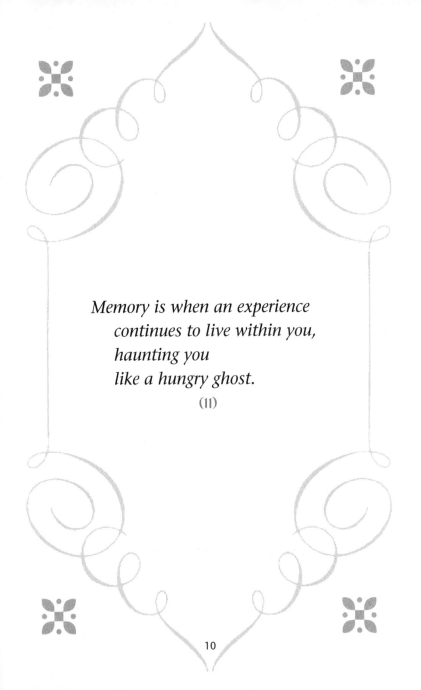

Memory is when an experience
continues to live within you,
haunting you
like a hungry ghost.

(11)

When you practice yoga and nonattachment,
   all the stories your mind creates
   through right knowledge,
   through wrong knowledge,
   through hearsay,
   through dreams,
   through memory . . .
   will dissolve
   like the images from a nightmare
   that quickly fades as you awaken.

(12)

Practice yoga and your
single-mindedness will increase.
Bending like a bamboo reed in the wind,
you will become steadfast
and grow roots that extend deep into the earth.

Devote yourself to yoga.
Watch your practice flourish.

(13 & 14)

Let go of your attachments
*   and discover self-mastery.*
Let go of your attachments.
Free yourself from desire.

(15)

The supreme nonattachment is
*   when you accept life as it is right now.*
Your mind's drama does not distract you
*   as you dwell in your True Self,*
*   needing nothing,*
*   wanting nothing.*

(16)

Samadhi brings four gifts
> *the gift of reasoning, or the ability to analyze . . .*
> *the gift of discernment, or the ability to see what*
>> *lies underneath the appearance of things . . .*
> *the gift of bliss . . .*
> *the gift of awareness of your True Self.*

(17)

*Samadhi allows you to break free
from the stories of your mind,
free from the tales of pain and loss that bind you.*

*Then, only the karma built up in previous lifetimes
can keep you tethered to the
struggle that many call life.*

(18)

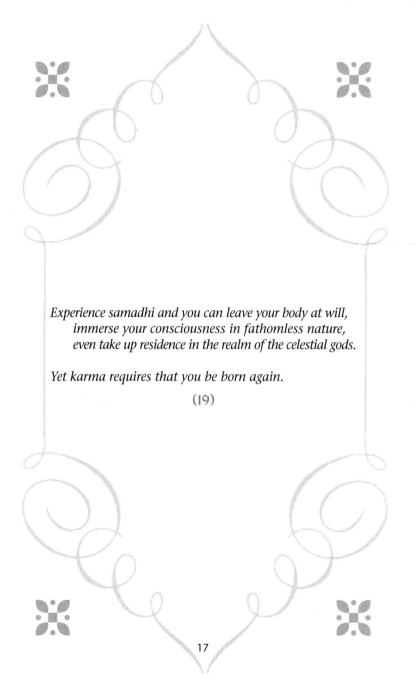

Experience samadhi and you can leave your body at will,
immerse your consciousness in fathomless nature,
even take up residence in the realm of the celestial gods.

Yet karma requires that you be born again.

(19)

To achieve samadhi
    you can draw upon faith
    or personal experience.
You can remember the nature of your True Self
    or contemplate your oneness with all of creation.
All four of these practices lead to samadhi.

The sincere intent to achieve samadhi
    will quickly bring you to this state of bliss.

(20 ε 21)

18

The more earnest your efforts,
and the more attention you
devote to your yoga practice,
the easier it is to attain samadhi.

(22)

*Surrender completely to Spirit
    and attain samadhi.
Spirit is the Supreme Self,
    the primordial yogi untouched by karma,
    free from desire,
    all-knowing.*

(23, 24, 25)

Spirit taught the greatest teachers directly.
Spirit dwells in timelessness,
   free from the past,
   free from the future.

(24, 25, 26)

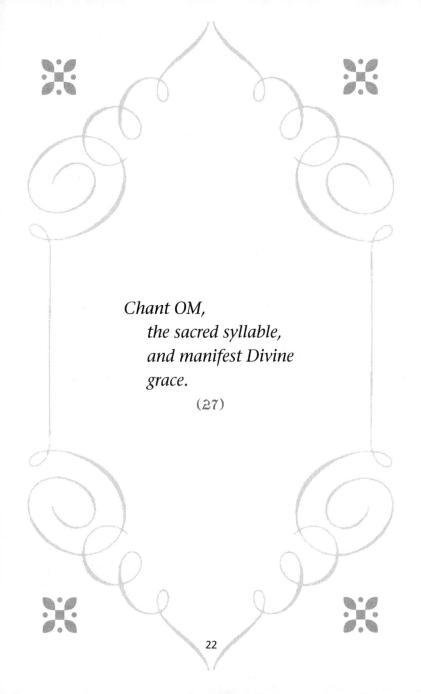

Chant OM,
the sacred syllable,
and manifest Divine
grace.

(27)

Chant OM.
Let it resonate
  within every cell
  in your heart, in your hands,
  and throughout your body.
Let it transform you
  at your very core.

(28)

Chant OM,
its sweet sound dissolving all obstacles,
clearing the fog of the mind,
revealing your Self.

(29)

Knowledge is hidden from us by clouds . . .
the clouds of
    sickness,
    doubt,
    laziness,
    lust,
    false perception,
    and the cloud of despair that arises
    when samadhi eludes you.

(30)

The clouds that obscure knowledge
*   disturb your breathing.*
Inhale
*   and notice your breath.*
Exhale
*   and blow away the grief,*
*   hopelessness, and fear.*
Breathe
*   and dispel the clouds.*

(31)

Still your mind
    and all clouds disappear.
Contemplate a single truth
    and clear sky appears.

(32)

So many ways to still the mind,
  make friends with those who live in joy,
  have compassion for those who suffer,
  delight in those who shine with virtue and integrity,
  turn your thoughts away from those who dwell in darkness.

(33)

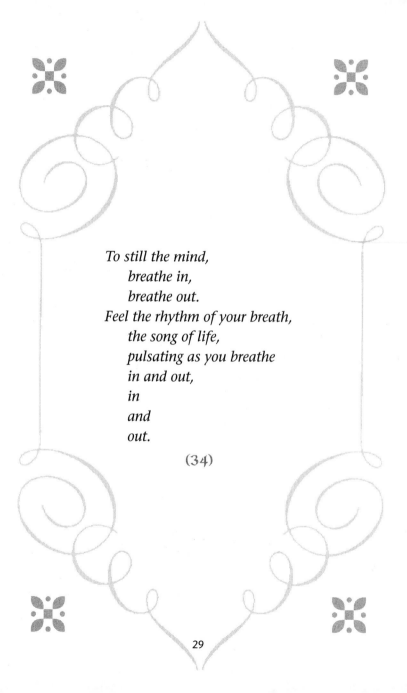

To still the mind,
  breathe in,
  breathe out.
Feel the rhythm of your breath,
  the song of life,
  pulsating as you breathe
  in and out,
  in
  and
  out.

(34)

Listen to the hidden sounds.
Use your other ears.
See the celestial sights.
Use your other eyes.
Perceive what cannot be
    measured by the ordinary senses.

(35)

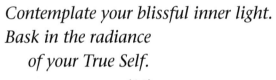

Contemplate your blissful inner light.
Bask in the radiance
of your True Self.

(36)

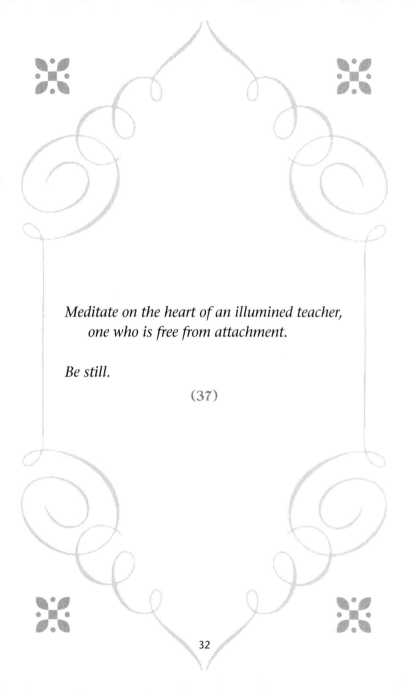

Meditate on the heart of an illumined teacher,
one who is free from attachment.

Be still.

(37)

Awaken.
Enter a land free of thought, of worry.
Focus on the dream from last night
    that lingers, moist and sticky on your pillow.
Meditate on one thing
    or another:
    a word, a color, a shape, a leaf.
Meditate on anything . . .
    it doesn't matter what . . .
    and still the mind.

(38 & 39)

In his gradual yet unstoppable way,
    the yogi gains mastery.
He meditates on a leaf
    and knows the complete forest.
She meditates on a flower
    and is awash in the scent of an entire meadow.
The yogi's meditation embraces
    a galaxy of stars,
    the atom,
    the sea,
    the planets.

(40)

Meditating by a lake,
    the yogi becomes the lake.
Meditating by a fire,
    the yogi becomes
    the flame,
    the crackling branch,
    the oak,
    the acorn.
She becomes one with the object of her meditation.
She becomes the red-rock canyon wall
    or soft and green like the moss.
She smells the rose and there is only the fragrance.
No thought of roses
She achieves samadhi.

(41)

Two kinds of samadhi are practiced on objects.

Practice samadhi
One with the object
    of contemplation.
One with the sun.
Become aware of the sun,
    our local star.

Practice samadhi.
One with the object
    of contemplation.
One with the sun.
Dissolve in the sun,
    only the sun.

bliss . . .

(42 & 43)

Underneath the moist, dark soil,
    the yogi discovers the source of creation,
    the Great Mother . . .
She who gave birth to the sun.

(44 & 45)

Be careful!
Practice nonattachment
*   lest samadhi cast you back into your story.*
Its seeds still bear the bitter fruit of karma.
Playing the role you have scripted,
*   playing the scene over,*
*   the dialogue is the same,*
*   the ending is the same.*

(46)

Free of attachment,
*   your True Self*
*   will shine in the purity of samadhi.*
Consciousness slices open the
*   underbelly of the night sky.*
Wisdom and truth spill out,
*   overflowing*
*   in a downpour of stars.*

(47 & 48)

The truth of wise teachers
*   and great books are gifts.*
The truth you discover
*   through reason is a treasure,*
*   but the most rare and precious jewel*
*   is the truth of experience.*

Experience samadhi.
Experience your True Self
*   and become truth itself.*

(49)

*Samadhi is like a rainstorm that washes away
all the stories from your past.
Everything dissolves and you perceive
only the primal substance of creation.*

(50)

When this storm has blown by
*   and not even the wind and the water remain,*
*   then this is the enduring samadhi.*

The ultimate samadhi
*   frees you of all stories,*
*   all karma.*
It bears no seeds.
It will bear no fruit.

(51)

REALIZATION,
OR THE
PRACTICE
OF YOGA

Allow your inner fire to purify you.
Let it blaze
    radiant,
        and watch all shadows disappear.
Accept what is.
Create no darkness, no pain.

Grow your spiritual practice.
Remember your light
    and surrender to Spirit.

This is Kriya yoga.

(1)

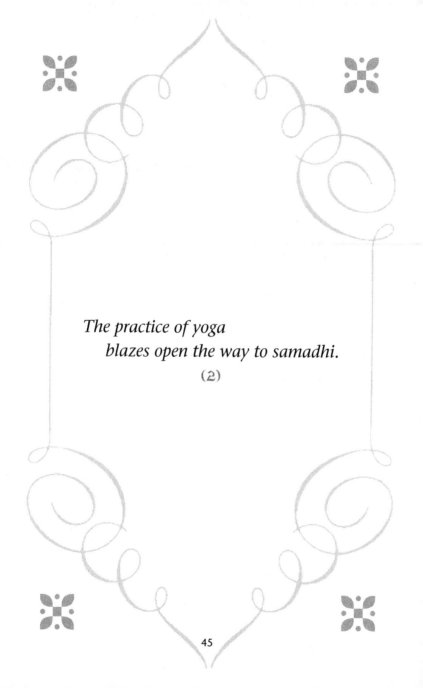

*The practice of yoga
    blazes open the way to samadhi.*

(2)

The five obstacles to samadhi are:
Ignorance
Egoism
Attachment
Anger
Fear of death.
Let go of your anger and your fear of death.
Let go of your attachments and your ego.
Release the thoughts that keep you from seeing
what fruits your actions will reap.

(3)

The obstacles to samadhi
    may lie dormant,
    but they can multiply like a weed
    creeping silently into your garden.
The obstacles to samadhi
    may appear suddenly one morning,
    choking your flowers
    and burrowing deep into the soil.

Ignorance allows them to flourish.

(4)

The ignorant man
  regards the impermanent as eternal,
  the impure as pure,
  the painful as pleasant,
  and the ego as God.

He worships the ego, and
  confuses his wounds for
  his inner wisdom and
  his mind for his True Self.

(5 & 6)

When your mind dwells on pain,
*   you are practicing attachment*
*   and you suffer.*
When your mind dwells on pleasure,
*   you are practicing attachment*
*   and you suffer.*
When your mind harbors anger and hatred,
*   you are practicing attachment.*
You become fettered to suffering.

(6, 7, 8)

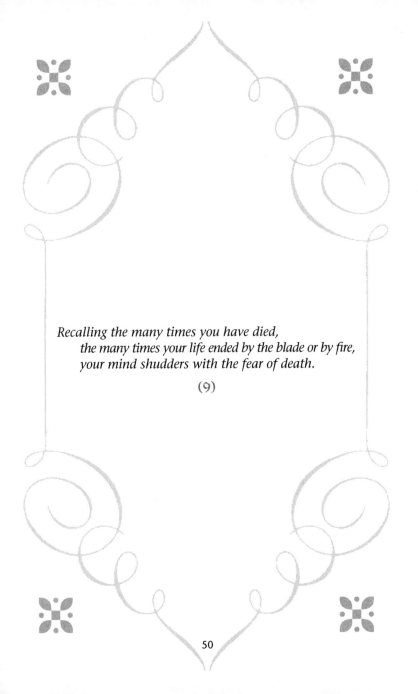

Recalling the many times you have died,
the many times your life ended by the blade or by fire,
your mind shudders with the fear of death.

(9)

*Weeds in the garden
     block you from samadhi.*

*When weeds are merely sprouting,
     you can uproot them easily.
Enter the stream of timelessness
     and observe as the weeds wither and die.*

*When your weeds are thick
     and deeply rooted,
     you must meditate.
Only then will they cease to grow.
Only then will they turn brown,
     decay,
     and return to the earth.*

(10 & 11)

51

Unaware and fearful of death,
you mistake the mind for the Self
and rage when you do not get your way.
The ego bristles.
You forge ahead,
intending to shake off your story and
leave it in the dust,
but it tags along behind you
from lifetime to lifetime.

Learn what you came to learn
or your story will greet you like a shadow,
attaching itself to you
every time you step into the sunlight.

(12)

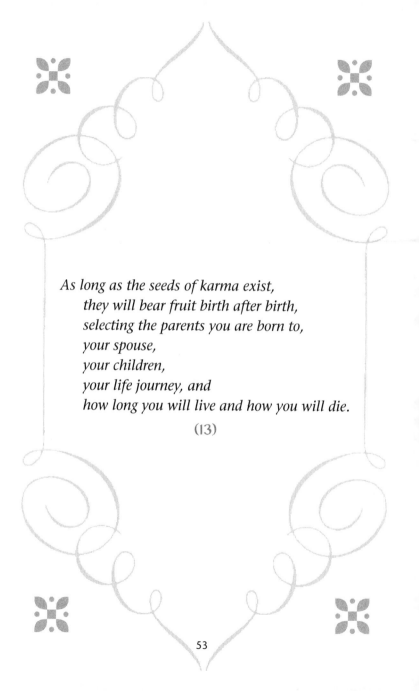

As long as the seeds of karma exist,
*   they will bear fruit birth after birth,*
*   selecting the parents you are born to,*
*   your spouse,*
*   your children,*
*   your life journey, and*
*   how long you will live and how you will die.*

(13)

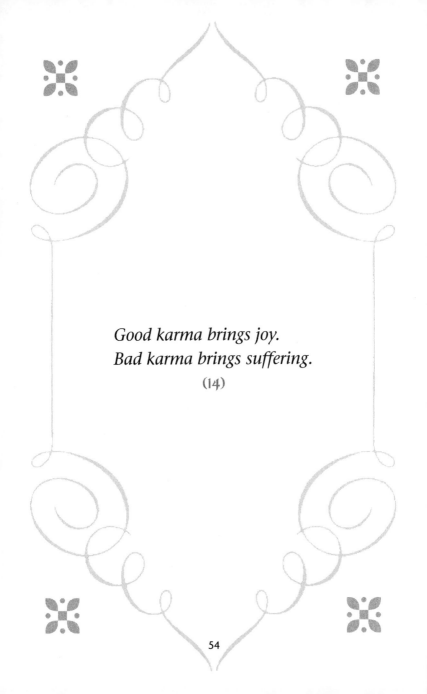

Good karma brings joy.
Bad karma brings suffering.

(14)

Karma is karma nonetheless.

Practice discernment
> *and you will see that even good karma is painful,*
> *for you already fear its loss.*
The fruits of good karma bring delight,
> *but they also bring fear*
> *as you imagine the tree no longer bearing sweet fruit.*

(15)

You can break the chains of karma.
Let them drop to the ground
   and walk free into the future.
No suffering.

(16)

We chain ourselves to suffering
  when we confuse the Seer for the seen,
  when we confuse the stories for the Storyteller.
Identify with your True Self
  and the chains of karma will drop away.

(17)

The True Self quietly observes the playground
where thoughts take form,
where games are played,
and the gunas obeyed.
These are the laws of light, activity, and inertia . . .
of inspiration, action, and obstacles.
The gunas are those things that can be known.
Your mind ponders all their qualities,
mistaking these for reality,
for they gave birth to the mind.
But the Self
remains unmoved by the
noise in the playground.

(18)

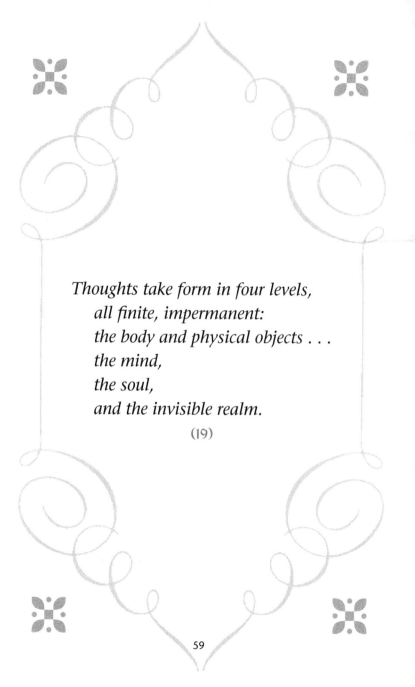

Thoughts take form in four levels,
  all finite, impermanent:
  the body and physical objects . . .
  the mind,
  the soul,
  and the invisible realm.

(19)

The True Self is infinite.
It knows no boundaries.
Pure essence,
    pure light,
    engulfing the mind, the soul,
    the body, the invisible realm
    with its radiance.

(20)

The True Self is the Seer,
*   observing all that can be known*
*   and all that remains unknowable . . .*
*   the visible and invisible worlds.*
These realms exist for the joy
*   and by the grace of the Seer.*

(21)

Upon awakening
    the Seer watches her dream dissipate
    like a wisp of a cloud.
Empty sky remains.

Those around him insist that the
    thunderclouds are overhead,
    cold and damp
    and trapped in a gray fog,
    but the Seer knows they are still asleep.

(22)

When the Seer identifies with the world,
*   others seem mighty and great.*
Wealth and power beckon to her.
She owns everything yet she has nothing.

This is caused by ignorance.

(23 & 24)

The wise woman does not confuse
     the road map with the road
     or indulge in dogmatic thinking.
She knows she can paint
     the ocean by dipping her brush in it,
     for she is the sea and the brush
     and the artist of her perceptions.

Heal your ignorance,
     discover your wisdom,
     awaken the Seer.

(24, 25, 26)

You gain knowledge in seven stages:
You realize that Spirit lives within you.
You recognize that suffering is optional.
You apprehend samadhi.
You learn to act with impeccable intent.
You grasp how the mind and the world exist,
    but only because you dream them into being.
You leave the playground of the gunas.
You apprehend your omniscience,
    your omnipresence.

(27)

Through the practice of yoga
you can awaken the Seer.
Let go of foolishness and confusion.
Look with the inner eyes.
Perceive all that you have missed.

(28)

Yoga is divided into eight limbs:
Yama: The Great Vows
Niyama: The Principles
Asana: The Postures
Pranayama: The Breathing Practice
Pratyahara: Turning Within
Dharana: Concentration
Dhyana: Meditation
Samadhi: Infinity

(29)

The Great Vows are:
Nonviolence . . .
    bring no harm to yourself or others.
Truthfulness . . .
    be true to your word, and let your word be true.
Integrity . . .
    do not steal; walk your talk.
Moderation . . .
    use wisely the life force within you.
Generosity . . .
    give more than you take,
    for nothing in the world really belongs to you.

No matter your name or your circumstances,
    no matter your age or the labels you affix to yourself,
    the great vows are universal.

(30 & 31)

The Principles are:
Practice purity . . .
    be unsullied by anger or vengeful thoughts.
Practice contentment . . .
    be at peace with what is and what is not.
Practice austerity . . .
    purify, reject greed, lack, and envy
    and the endless desire for more.
Study . . .
    and cultivate wisdom.
Open your heart to all that can be known.
Surrender . . .
    become one with Spirit,
    aware of your sacred nature.
Know that you are woven into the
    intricate matrix of creation.

(32)

When you find your mind
wandering away from yoga,
do not fight it.
Think something beautiful instead.

(33)

The greatest failings are harming others
and not speaking the truth.
These always result in suffering.
They are caused by anger and desire.
Remember this.

(34)

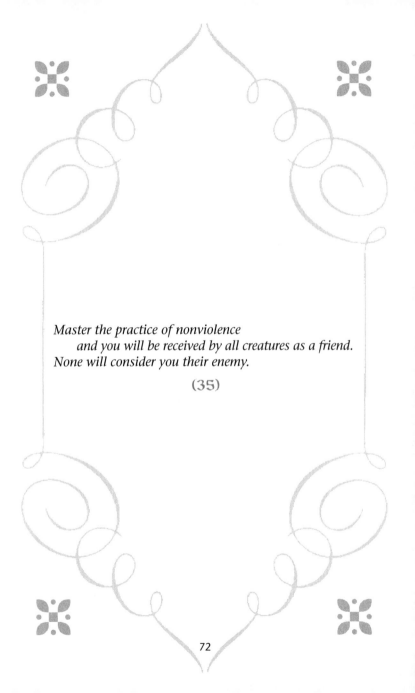

Master the practice of nonviolence
*   and you will be received by all creatures as a friend.*
None will consider you their enemy.

(35)

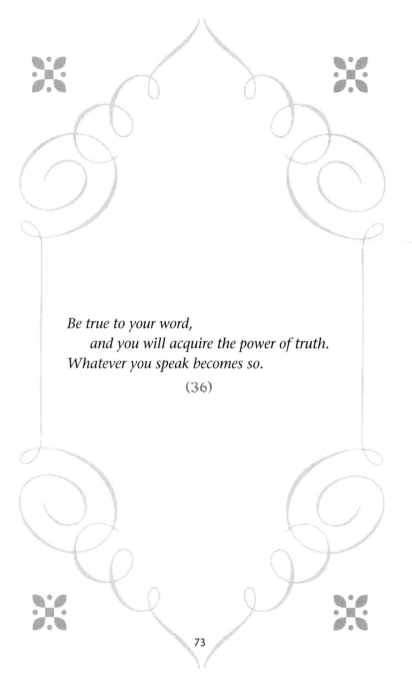

Be true to your word,
and you will acquire the power of truth.
Whatever you speak becomes so.

(36)

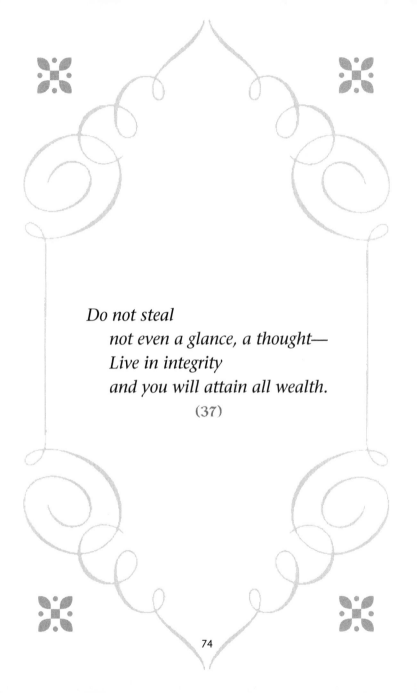

Do not steal
> *not even a glance, a thought—*
> *Live in integrity*
> *and you will attain all wealth.*

(37)

Practice moderation,
    employ your sexual energy wisely.
Squander nothing,
    and you will acquire spiritual power.

(38)

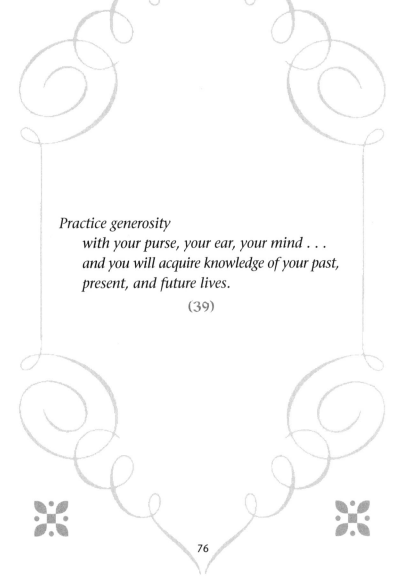

*Practice generosity
    with your purse, your ear, your mind . . .
    and you will acquire knowledge of your past,
    present, and future lives.*

(39)

Practice purity,
   lose your fascination with your body
   and the physical form of others.
You will perceive beauty with different eyes.

(40)

When purity goes below the skin and
penetrates to the essence of your being,
you will no longer be in the grip of your passions.
Your heart becomes pure,
your mind innocent,
your concentration effortless,
and your inner vision clear.

(41)

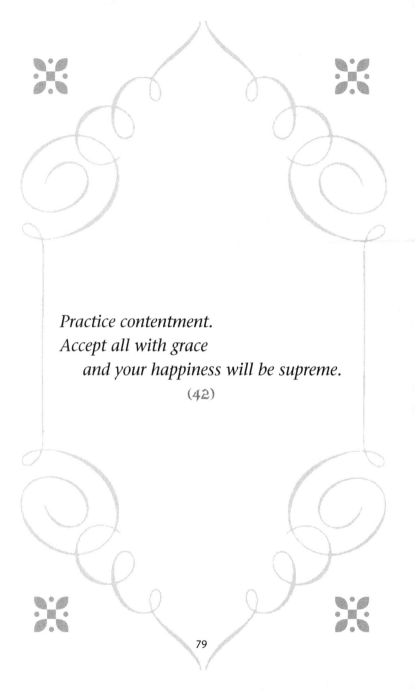

Practice contentment.
Accept all with grace
and your happiness will be supreme.

(42)

Practice austerity.
Remove impurities from your food,
*   your air, and the water you drink.*
Your body is purified
*   and you develop the siddhis.*
You see the storm brewing while it is still a
*   whisper on the wing of a butterfly.*
You heal the sorrow in the heart of your ancestors.

Your strength and endurance are beyond measure.

(43)

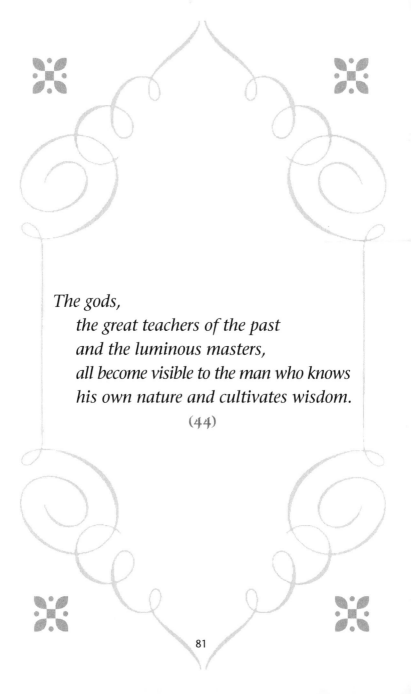

The gods,
the great teachers of the past
and the luminous masters,
all become visible to the man who knows
his own nature and cultivates wisdom.

(44)

Spirit is your source
*   and the cause of all your actions.*

Understand this and you attain samadhi.

(45)

Steady in your intention,
*   you'll be steady in your posture.*
Asana can come naturally.

(46)

Without effort,
  asana becomes perfect.
Stop trying.
Let yourself soar,
  a bird carried on the wind.

  (47)

Nothing can disturb your practice . . .
  neither heat nor cold,
  hard nor soft,
  not too much or too little . . .
  no more dualities.

All is right
  just as it is.

(48)

Master asana,
be aware of your breath,
your lungs as you fill them,
breathing deeply.
Deeply
sustaining your breath,
easily
drink in this life force.

(49)

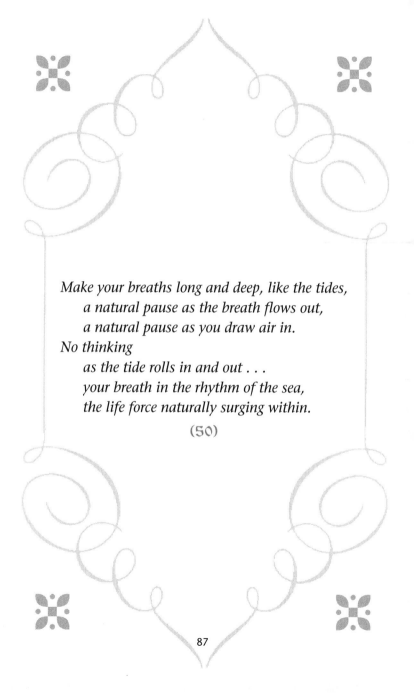

Make your breaths long and deep, like the tides,
a natural pause as the breath flows out,
a natural pause as you draw air in.
No thinking
as the tide rolls in and out . . .
your breath in the rhythm of the sea,
the life force naturally surging within.

(50)

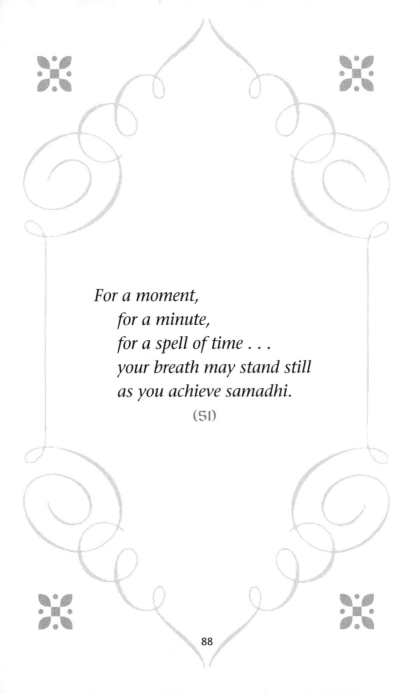

For a moment,
for a minute,
for a spell of time . . .
your breath may stand still
as you achieve samadhi.

(51)

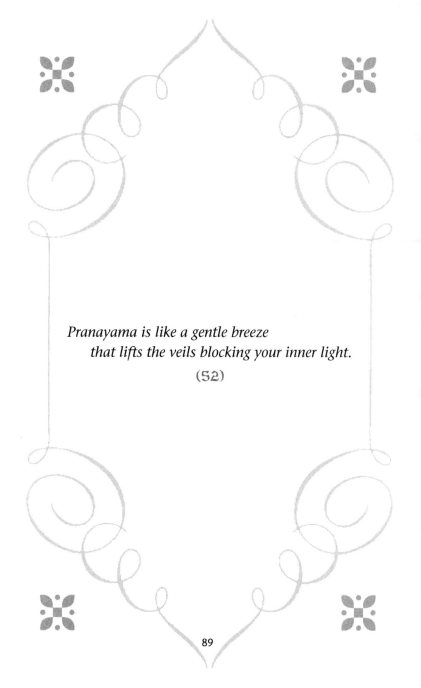

*Pranayama is like a gentle breeze
that lifts the veils blocking your inner light.*

(52)

Breathe.
Experience the life force
and you will become steadfast,
able to concentrate.
Empty mind.

(53)

When the mind no longer darts
from one object to another,
one thought to another
a bird alighting on one branch, then the next,
then it is free to turn within,
like a turtle withdrawing into its shell.
This is pratyahara.

(54)

Attain mastery of the senses
*   and they will no longer púll you*
*   this way and that.*
Sights no longer call to you,
*   yearning for your attention.*
Sounds no longer beckon you.
Tastes do not fascinate you or make you wince.

You experience yourself and the world
*   as if for the first time.*

(55)

THE SIDDHIS,
OR THE
MAGICAL POWERS

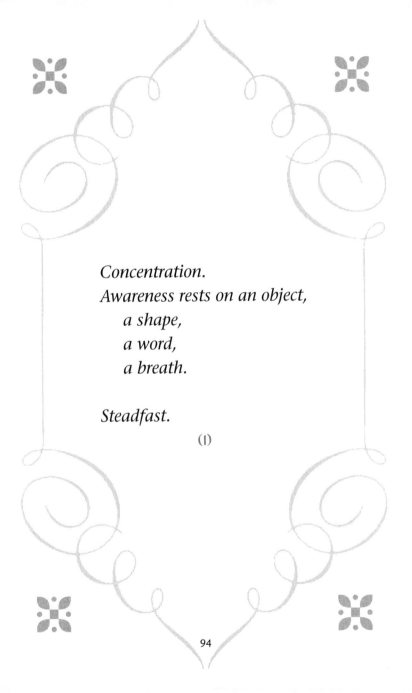

Concentration.
Awareness rests on an object,
  a shape,
  a word,
  a breath.

Steadfast.

(1)

Meditation.
Awareness fixes gently on an object or a breath,
*   unmoved by thoughts that wander by.*
Conscious only of this.

Unwavering.

(2)

Samadhi.
Immersed in concentration and meditation,
all thoughts and distractions far away.
Your focus steady,
you achieve samadhi.
All that exists is the heart of the experience.
There is no one meditating,
no one concentrating,
only awareness.

There is no yogi,
only the yoga.

(3)

Clear and lucid, practice
    concentration,
    meditation,
    samadhi.
This is samyana.
Practice this when you awaken,
    when you sleep,
    when you dream.
Then the light of wisdom grows,
    illuminating the way to
    even higher states of being.

(4, 5, 6)

Unlike the other limbs of yoga
  concentration, meditation, and samadhi
  are practiced within one's self.
Yet once you taste the ultimate samadhi
  where the seeds of karma cease to exist,
  even these practices will seem external.

I have ceased to exist.

(7 & 8)

In samyana, memories rise to the surface,
dissolve naturally,
yet leave tiny ripples in the awareness
that radiate outward toward the shore
until the surface smoothes itself.
Mind and awareness merge
again in stillness.

(9)

In stillness
    true power requires no exertion,
    no effort.
Simply practice yoga.
    Then awareness will cease to waver,
    untouched by the swirling winds of
    thought, worry, and desire.

(10)

Be still and in samadhi
and your eyes will open.
You will see the birth of the galaxies
and the death of the universe.
You may even be swept up in the
astral river of infinity,
gulping mouthfuls of timelessness,
swallowing past and future in the same instant.

(11 & 12)

Immersed in this river of timelessness,
    you will come to know the secrets of nature,
    understand transformation,
    from larva to cocoon to butterfly . . .
    from acorn to oak . . .
    and recognize the matrix of a tree,
    which resides in the unseen world.

You will solve the riddles of how
    time flows in more than one direction,
    and unravel the mysteries etched in layers of stone,

    ash, and bone deep within the earth.

(13 & 14)

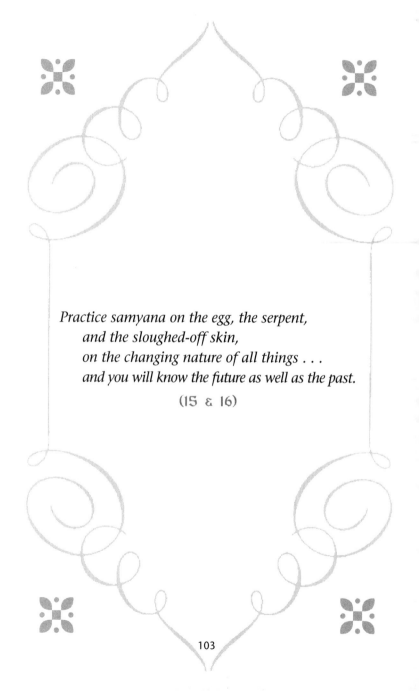

Practice samyana on the egg, the serpent,
  and the sloughed-off skin,
  on the changing nature of all things . . .
  and you will know the future as well as the past.

(15 & 16)

Hear the call of the loon resounding across the lake.
Practice samyana on its haunting cry
*   and you will understand its language.*
Know that it is flirting with its mate
*   or singing in joy.*
Practice samyana on your lover's words
*   and you will not confuse her*
*   speech with what she is telling you*
*   in her heart.*

(17)

The specters of former lives
    are dim apparitions that float through your mind.
They can be seen clearly when you practice samyana.
Your stories will appear on their faces,
    memories from every one of your past lifetimes.
You will remember everything that you have forgotten.

(18)

Look upon another.
Practice samyana on his grimace or his smile,
    the straightening of shoulders,
    his walk,
    and you will understand what is in the mind of that person,
    but the secrets of his heart will remain hidden.

(19 & 20)

Practice samyana on the form of your body,
the curve of your leg,
the outline of your fingers,
and you can become invisible,
no longer seen by others
beyond the perception of the senses.

Enter a room and you are noticed
when you choose to be seen,
unheard,
unfelt,
yet in full mastery of the light and
power emanating from you.

(21 & 22)

The stories of your past will be retold today
    or in another lifetime
    when your karma manifests.
Practice samyana on the memories of your past lives
    on the memories of your past deaths.
Practice samyana on the signs of your mortality.

You will master how and when this lifetime will end
    and be prepared to meet infinity.

(23)

Practice samyana on love or compassion,
virtue or creativity,
and these qualities will be yours to use,
yours to bestow
on whomever may need them.

(24)

Practice samyana on the strength of elephants
and you will stomp on obstacles as
if they were mere blades of grass.
Acquire strength of the heart and soul.
Practice samyana on the creatures of
the forest and the mountain.
Try on their wings, their vision, their instincts,
until they become yours.

(25)

Practice samyana on your inner radiance
and you will gain wisdom.
Secrets will reveal themselves.
You will know about each drop of water
and the cloud that holds them.
Nothing will be too small or too large for you to grasp.
You will know why the rain clouds are not in the sky
and how to call them back.
You will know that there are
showers in the valley miles away.

You will know this because
far away and near have ceased to exist for you.

(26)

Practice samyana on the sun,
    and you will know the seven heavenly realms,
    the six hells and the netherworlds.
Practice samyana on the moon,
    and you will know every star.
Practice samyana on the North Star
    and you will know the heart of the Milky Way,
    the far-off galaxies
    and the journey of the planets.

(27, 28, 29)

Practice samyana on the chakra at your navel.
See inside your body or that of someone else.
You will know the workings of each organ
    and the health of your body or hers.
Practice samyana on the chakra at your throat . . .
    slake your thirst and sate your hunger.
Practice samyana on the hollow below your throat
    and as you meditate you will feel yourself relax.

Practice samyana on the light above your head
    and you will perceive the luminous ones,
    the angels and the masters.

(30, 31, 32, 33)

Gradually
or in the flash of an instant,
one can achieve the siddhis
and all the hidden knowledge is revealed.

(34)

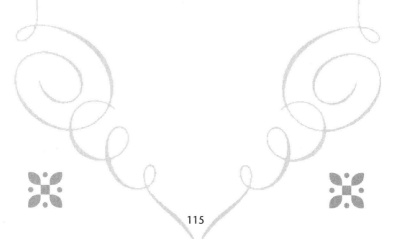

*Practice samyana on the heart chakra
and know pure mind.*

(35)

The mind and the Self must not be confused,
for the mind is fleeting and temporary
and is meant to serve its master.
When you confuse the Self for the mind,
you suffer.

Practice samyana on the distinction
between the mind and the Self
and you will dwell in your divinity.

Once you know you are a
spiritual being in a body,
a visitor in this world,
you will never again
need a spiritual experience.

(36)

Clearly distinguishing between the mind and the Self,
    you become enlightened in an instant.
All powers are bestowed upon you,
    perceiving beyond the senses.
Stepping outside of time,
    you experience the past and the future.
Enjoy the gift of the siddhis.
You have achieved perfection.

If you swell with pride over these powers,
    you will be held back from the higher levels of samadhi.
If you fear these powers and renounce them,
    you will be held back from the higher levels of samadhi.

(37 & 38)

Unfetter your awareness from your body,
soar free of time and place.
You may settle softly into the body of another,
seeing, feeling, sensing as they do;
or simply sail through the sky,
dipping and gliding.
Master the luminous body.
You can become weightless,
rising like a leaf on an autumn breeze,
or walk across a pond,
leaving your body on the shore.
Free of the weight of the body,
you can master the moment of your death.

(39 & 40)

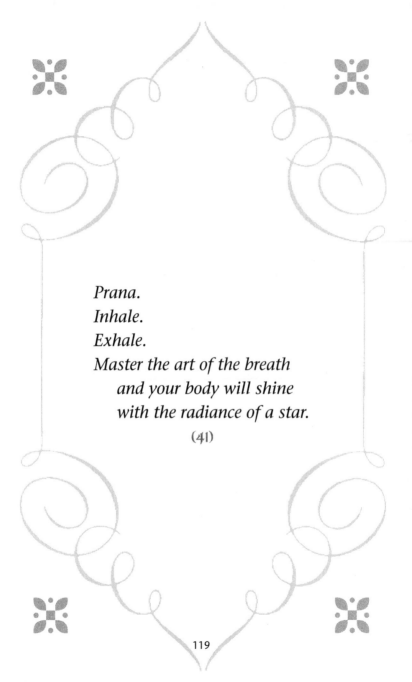

Prana.
Inhale.
Exhale.
Master the art of the breath
and your body will shine
with the radiance of a star.

(41)

Practice samyana and listen
across the vastness of time and space.
You will recall the tales told by the
fireside long ago,
as well as the stories not yet told,
sitting with the ancestors
and walking with your children's children.

(42)

Practice samyana on the immensity
of time and space.
You will be able to revisit the past
and heal the future.

(43)

Loosened from the grip of the body,
awareness rises.
Practice samyana on this freedom
and all veils that conceal the
light of your True Self are destroyed.

(44)

Practice samyana on the flames,
the embers,
and the nature of fire.
Practice samyana on the damp soil
and its power to transform a seed into a tree.
Practice samyana on the wind and the
laughter and sadness it carries
in the scent of a wildflower.
Practice samyana on the water of the
creek as it trickles over stones,
bringing life to the roots of the grasses.

Then you will have gained
mastery over all the elements of creation:
earth, air, fire, water . . .
space-time.

(45)

Embracing these powers,
mastering the elements,
traveling through time and space,
the yogi can fashion a new body for himself . . .
one that ages, heals, and dies differently.

(46)

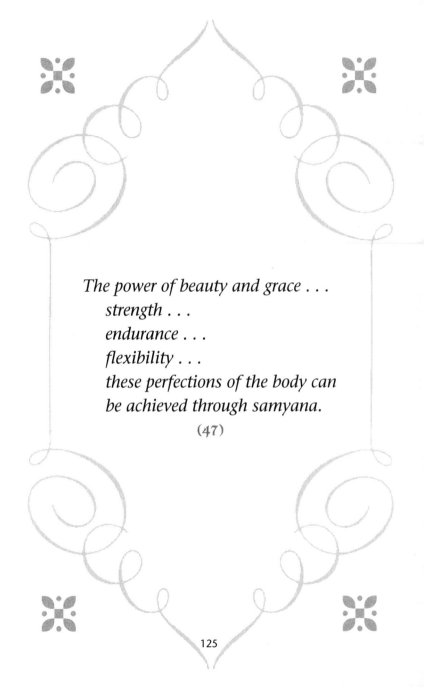

The power of beauty and grace . . .
    strength . . .
    endurance . . .
    flexibility . . .
    these perfections of the body can
    be achieved through samyana.

        (47)

Practice samyana on your perception,
on your vision,
on your hearing,
on all your senses and their qualities.
You will know the taste of the salt of the ocean
even while in the desert.
You will know the sound of a crackling fire
even while swimming in the sea.

You will know that you are
dreaming the world into being
and that it is dreaming you.

(48)

Know that all you perceive is real,
that it exists because you perceive it.
Then the world mirrors perfectly the
condition of your love and your intent.
You can travel at the speed of the mind,
faster than light.
You can feel the warmth of the jaguar's breath
though you are miles away.
You have mastered your inner nature.
You perceive with hidden senses
and know that you, too, are the jaguar,
the rain forest,
and that you and I have never been apart.

(49)

The mind, a grain of sand,
the Self, the beach.
The mind is a single note made by a flute,
the Self, the breath,
the wind.

Practice samyana on the difference,
then all wisdom and power flow into you.

(50)

Employ the spiritual powers
to attain samadhi,
then let them slip to the ground
like the walking stick you discard at the end of the path.
Stride free, leaving the woods behind you,
knowing the stick will be there upon your return,
should you need it.

(51)

When on the way, you encounter an angel
who sits at your table and shines her light upon your face,
attend to your supper
and the business she has with you.
Should you become drunk with awe instead
and find your mind burdened
with even a thought or two of this special moment,
you will miss the blessing the angel has come to bestow.

(52)

Practice samyana on one instant
and you will know the measure of the present.
Your eyes will be open to colors no one else sees.
Possibilities and journeys that no one has imagined.

You will understand that you do not cross the same river twice,
not even once.

(53)

Knowing the river and the mountain,
    the shore and the horizon at once,
    and every facet of the Divine, the unmanifest,
    at once
    the yogi simply knows,
    understands effortlessly,
    she is free.

(54)

This is absolute freedom.
When the mind is swept clean of all the cobwebs
     and becomes pure, like the Self,
     a still pool that reflects everything,
     mirrors the world back to itself
     perfectly.

(55)

IV

ABSOLUTE FREEDOM

The yogi achieves spiritual power in five ways:
By drinking from the spring that sources from
his yoga practice in former lifetimes.
By tasting the special herbs that carry him
out of his ordinary consciousness,
for they are infused with power.
By chanting mantras that travel over
valleys and foothills,
By purifying his body as he practices austerity.
By practicing samadhi.

(I)

Open yourself to the wisdom of nature,
vast and expansive,
bringing forth life in myriad ways.
Let its intelligence inform you
and transform you.
Let nature help you evolve into a higher being.

(2)

Evolution guides your destiny and mine.
Your nature is to grow and change,
*   to become greater and wiser,*
*   deeper and richer.*
Growth is like a rushing river.
Boulders may slow its path
*   or redirect its flow,*
*   but they cannot stop its currents.*

When the farmer removes stones from the creek,
*   its waters seep into every corner of his fields.*

(3)

You are not of one mind.
You are of many minds,
 each created by the Self.
A mind that is forgiving and compassionate.
A mind that is confused and suspicious.
A mind that pretends to know all
 but is only a foolish monkey,
 hopping from rock to tree and back again.

(4)

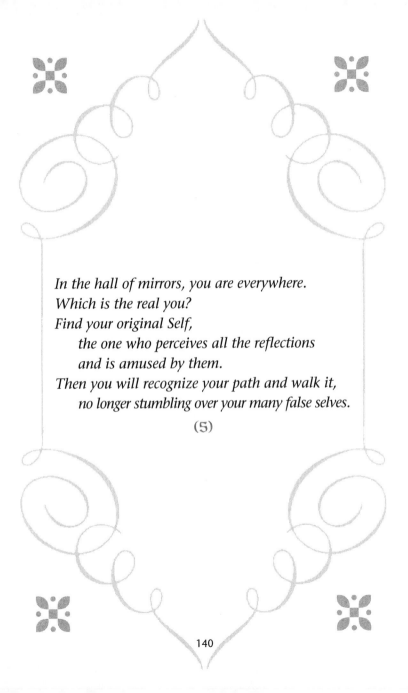

In the hall of mirrors, you are everywhere.
Which is the real you?
Find your original Self,
the one who perceives all the reflections
and is amused by them.
Then you will recognize your path and walk it,
no longer stumbling over your many false selves.

(5)

Practice samadhi
> and your mind will be free at last,
> free to close the storybook.

The tales of terror,
> the enchanting yarns spun on
> long winter evenings,
> the thrilling adventures and promised treasures . . .
> you will not be in any of them.

(6)

Those who do not practice yoga are caught up in intricate plots.
Some are cast in a heroic drama, others in a tale of suffering.
Their karma may be good, bad, or a little of each.
But the yogi's journey is neither comic nor tragic,
     good nor bad.
It simply is.

(7)

In every garden, the seeds of karma will sprout.
The gardener may be a man in this lifetime,
a woman in the next.
Today or tomorrow
the same plants will grow their bitter fruit
even when the seeds fall from the fur of a creature
who sows them unknowingly as he trots across your meadow.

Karma will grow and bear fruit
when the conditions are right.

(8 ε 9)

Always
you have chosen life,
breathing without thinking,
pulling yourself out from the ocean,
filling your lungs with air,
learning to walk on the earth.
Before the first cell divided,
before you inhabited your form,
you chose life.

So, too, karma has always existed . . .
before time
and after time,
entwined with life
with cause and effect,
with mind and desire.

(10)

Look beyond past and future.
Perceive that tomorrow affects today
and that all events unfold exactly as they should.
Let go of your need to orchestrate your life
and your karma will dissolve.

(11)

Caught in the stories of karma,
*   you perceive past and future as real.*
Free yourself from karma
*   and tomorrow dissolves into yesterday.*
Your hapless stories and noble battles
*   will no longer be retold.*

(12)

The form and expression of karma will vary,
*   sometimes obvious, sometimes subtle.*
You may think
*   you have never experienced these sagas before.*
Karma is a play with a well-worn script.
Inspiration, action, and obstacles determine its plot.
You confuse it for reality.

(13 & 14)

One man touches the trunk
  and pronounces the elephant long like a snake.
One man touches the tusk
  and pronounces the elephant sharp
  like a sword.
One man touches the tail
  and pronounces the elephant wispy
  like a broom.
The mind perceives as if it were a blind man,
  relying on its limited senses.
Become one with the elephant.
Dissolve the mind
  and know the beast's true nature.

(15)

What you perceive exists even
   when you close your eyes
   or when you do not sense its presence.
The world is real.
Its nature is separate
   from your mind and your thoughts.

(16)

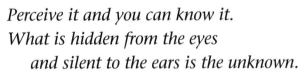

Perceive it and you can know it.
What is hidden from the eyes
*   and silent to the ears is the unknown.*

(17)

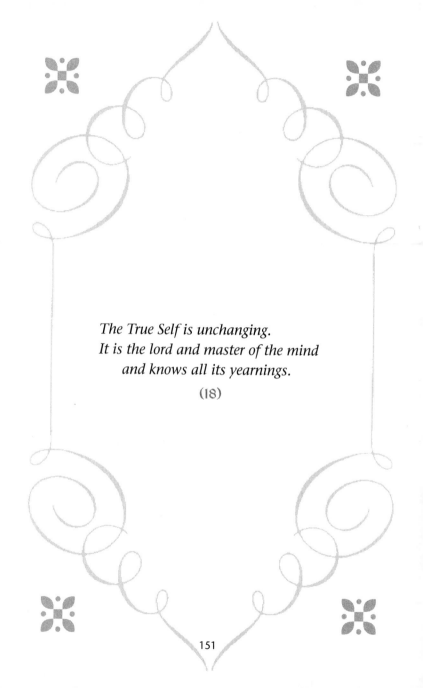

The True Self is unchanging.
It is the lord and master of the mind
and knows all its yearnings.

(18)

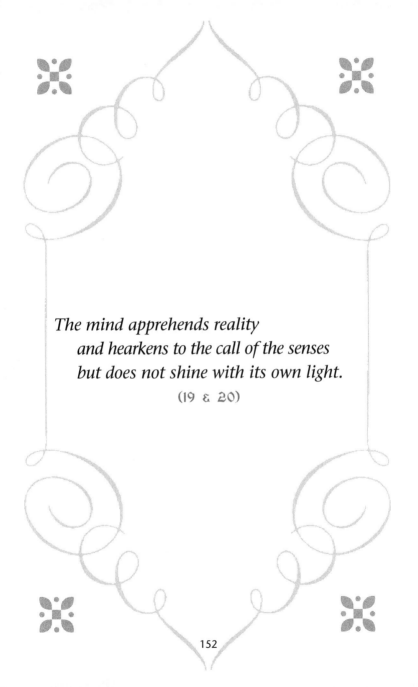

The mind apprehends reality
and hearkens to the call of the senses
but does not shine with its own light.

(19 & 20)

If your mind perceived all that surrounds it,
you would need a second mind to perceive the first
and another to perceive the second,
like an endless number of reflections,
creating a massive confusion of memories.

(21)

Pure and unchanging,
the True Self is unmoved by the mind.
When the mind turns away from the
fleeting distractions of sensation,
it acquires the form of the True Self.
Then the mind observes all that surrounds it
and can observe the one who Sees.
Able to perceive the Seer
and understand all.

(22 & 23)

*The mind is the gardener
    sowing the seeds of karma,
    duty-bound to plant according
    to the will of the True Self,
    the master it serves.
The yogi no longer confuses the
    gardener for the master.
He is discerning
    and he attains liberation.*

(24, 25, 26)

Should you fail to practice discernment
   distracted by the novelties that tease the senses,
   the karma from your past will spill over into now.
Practice samadhi.
Remove all obstacles
   and ignore the enticing offers
   from the playground of the mind.

(27 & 28)

The glory bestowed upon you
  can distract you from your practice.
Remain steadfast and discerning
  even as praise and wealth are laid at your feet
  and you will float above these riches
  on a cloud of virtue.
Suffering will end and karma will cease.
Knowledge will no longer be distorted by
  the smudged lens of perception.
Limitless wisdom will fill you,
  coming not from a book or a teacher
  but directly from your experience.

(29, 30, 31)

Practice samadhi
 and the dance of action and reaction,
 inspiration and discouragement,
 suffering and joy,
 will end,
 for they will have served their purpose.

(32)

*Time is the uninterrupted sequence of
      transformations of the gunas.
You understand this when you
      step outside of time, into infinity.*

*Observe as the dancers intertwine,
      weaving the timeline that stretches from past to
      future with their serpentine movements.
Watch from the banks of the river of infinity,
      which flows in all directions,
      no longer following the steps of the dancers.
Shining forth in brilliance,
      lord of the dance,
      your true nature is revealed
      and you are free.*

(33 & 34)

GLOSSARY

asana: A posture, to be held steadily and comfortably; literally, *asana* means "seat," and it refers not only to physical posture, but to meditation.

ekagrata: Single-mindedness; sustained concentration on one thing.

gunas: Qualities of natural phenomena; the aspects of objects in the material world. The three gunas are rajas (active), sattva (in balance), and tamas (inactive).

jivamukta: A liberated soul that is still connected to the body.

kundalini: The power of spiritual awakening, symbolized by a coiled snake located at the base of the spine; the force of spiritual maturation.

maya: The illusion of the material world.

prana: The breath or life force.

pranayama: Control of the breath; rhythmic, deep breathing that gives yogis control over their life force.

pratyahara: A turning within; a level of awareness at which yoga practitioners no longer engage the messages from their senses, having withdrawn from the material world.

rishi: A sage or ascetic who perceives the sacred; a saint.

sadhu: A renunciate yogi or ascetic practitioner of yoga and meditation.

samadhi: The state of ecstatic bliss achieved through the practice of yoga.

samyana: The state in which one is practicing concentration, meditation, and samadhi all at the same time; simultaneously experiencing focused attention, awareness, and energy.

shakti: The creative force of the Divine feminine.

siddhis: "Perfections"; spiritual powers, such as physic abilities and the ability to travel outside of one's body.

❀ ❀ ❀ ❀

ACKNOWLEDGMENTS

The co-creators of this book are the original yogis of the Himalayas, who 50,000 years ago settled in Siberia and then traversed the Bering Strait into North America. These individuals were my teachers' teachers, and I am in their debt for the knowledge that they so graciously shared with me in the 25 years that I trained with the medicine men and women of the Americas.

During my visit to the source of the Ganges, I met many individuals who inspired me and contributed to this work. First and foremost is my friend Shyamdas, poet extraordinaire; and Vishnu Shastri Punditji, Sanskrit scholar and grammarian from Mathura. Without their guidance and deft deciphering of the subtle Sanskrit passages of Patanjali's text, this book would not have been possible.

I would like to thank Reid Tracy at Hay House for the opportunity to publish this work. To my editor Nancy Peske, I owe my gratitude for her wit, poetry, and wisdom. Susan Reiner helped me stay on track with the essence of the feminine teachings. My editor at Hay House, Jill Kramer, has been a steward of the project from the start. My friend Ganga White helped guide me through the maze of thoughts and opinions about the Yoga Sutras.

This is not an academic version of the Yoga Sutras. There are many excellent translations of Patanjali available, and I would recommend to those seeking a more scholarly version that they consult the very fine renditions from Georg Feuerstein and Douglas Brooks. I encourage you to keep a copy of these translations on your bookshelf. I consulted many translations of Patanjali for this project. Decades ago I became enthralled with Swami Pradhavananda and Christopher Isherwood's translation. I also consulted Swami Satchidananda's version, as well as the excellent, if obtuse, translation by Rama Prasada with a commentary by Vyasa from the turn of the last century.

Last, I owe my gratitude to Swami Muktananda, who blessed me with his Shaktipat nearly 30 years ago; and Don Antonio Morales, who shared the Munay-Ki. Their energetic transmissions were the yogic gifts of power and grace that fueled this project.

❀ ❀ ❀ ❀

ABOUT THE AUTHOR

Alberto Villoldo, Ph.D., a psychologist and medical anthropologist, has studied the spiritual practices of the Amazon and the Andes for more than 25 years. While at San Francisco State University, he founded the Biological Self-Regulation Laboratory to study how the mind creates psychosomatic health and disease.

Dr. Villoldo directs The Four Winds Society, where he instructs individuals throughout the world in the practice of energy medicine and soul retrieval. He has training centers in New England; California; the U.K.; the Netherlands; and Park City, Utah.

An avid skier, hiker, and mountaineer, he leads annual expeditions to the Amazon and the Andes to work with the wisdom teachers of the Americas.

Website: **www.thefourwinds.com**

❀ ❀ ❀ ❀

NOTES

NOTES

NOTES

NOTES

NOTES

NOTES

Hay House Titles of Related Interest

❀ ❀ ❀

All of the above are available at your local bookstore,
or may be ordered by contacting Hay House (see last page).

❀ ❀ ❀

We hope you enjoyed this Hay House book.
If you'd like to receive a free catalog featuring
additional Hay House books and products, or if you'd
like information about the Hay Foundation, please contact:

Hay House, Inc.
P.O. Box 5100
Carlsbad, CA 92018-5100

(760) 431-7695 or **(800) 654-5126**
(760) 431-6948 (fax) or **(800) 650-5115 (fax)**
www.hayhouse.com® • **www.hayfoundation.org**

Tune in to **HayHouseRadio.com®** for the best in inspirational
talk radio featuring top Hay House authors! And, sign up via the
Hay House USA Website to receive the Hay House online newsletter
and stay informed about what's going on with your favorite authors.
You'll receive bimonthly announcements about Discounts and Offers,
Special Events, Product Highlights, Free Excerpts, Giveaways, and more!
www.hayhouse.com®